BIG BU$INE$$

Disney

Adam Sutherland

First published in 2012 by Wayland

Wayland
338 Euston Road
London NW1 3BH

Wayland Australia
Level 17/207 Kent Street
Sydney, NSW 2000

Commissioning editor: Joyce Bentley
Designer: Emma Randall
Picture researcher: Shelley Noronha

Acknowledgements: The author and publisher would like to thank the following for allowing their pictures to be reproduced in this publication: Cover: © Purestock / Alamy; title page: The Granger Collection / Topfoto; p4 Disney Enterprises / TopFoto; p5 Pierre Verdy/AFP/Getty Images; Time & Life Pictures/Getty Images; p7 The Granger Collection / TopFoto; p8 © Photoshot; p9 David McNew/Getty Images; p10 The Granger Collection / TopFoto; p11, p12 Everett Collection/Rex Features; p13 WpN/Photoshot; p14 Disney/Ronald Grant Archive/TopFoto; p15 Yale Joel//Time Life Pictures/Getty Images; p16 Stewart Cook/Rex Features; p17 © Photoshot; p18 Ron Galella/WireImage; p19 Barry King/Liaison; p20 ©Monika Graff/The Image Works; p21 Phil McCarten/Reuters/Corbis; p22 WpN/UPPA/Photoshot; p24 Disney Parks via Getty Images; p25 Industrial Light & Magic. © 2008 MVLFFLLC. ™ & © 2008 Marvel Entertainment. All rights reserved. © TopFoto.co.uk; p26 © Photoshot; p27 India Today Group/Getty Images; p32 The Granger Collection / Topfoto

British Library Cataloguing in Publication Data:
Sutherland, Adam.
Disney. -- (Big business)
1. Walt Disney Company--Juvenile literature. 2. Motion
picture industry--United States --Juvenile literature.
I. Title II. Series
338.4'779143-dc23

ISBN: 978 0 7502 6922 3

Printed in China
Wayland is a division of Hachette Children's Books, an Hachette UK company.
www.hachette.co.uk

Contents

Disney on top 4

The birth of Mickey Mouse 6

Snow White and the seven Oscars 8

Disney in your living room 10

The birth of the theme parks 12

Life and death at Disney 14

The wonderful world of Disney 16

Disney grows up 18

'The best 30 minutes of a child's day' 20

Disney gets interactive 22

Steadying the ship 24

What does the future hold for Disney? 26

Invent the next Disney theme park ride 28

SWOT analysis 29

Do you have what it takes to work at Disney?   30

Glossary 31

Index 32

Disney on top

The Walt Disney Company is one of the best known, best loved and, just as importantly, most successful companies on the planet. In 2011, the latest instalment in the hit film series _Pirates of the Caribbean: On Stranger Tides_, starring Johnny Depp as pirate Jack Sparrow, passed $1 billion (£643m) in ticket sales worldwide and became the eighth highest grossing film ever released. (The _Pirates_ franchise is based on a popular ride, opened nearly 50 years earlier in 1967, at Disneyland Park in Anaheim, California.)

And it wasn't just at the box office that Disney had a bumper year. Walt Disney Parks and Resorts worldwide brought in nearly $12 billion (£7.7bn), with revenue from TV networks, including sports network ESPN, Disney Channel and ABC Family contributing a further $19 billion (£12.2bn) to Disney's coffers.

With total 2011 revenues of $40.9bn (£26.3bn), and net profits of $4.8bn (£3.1bn) Disney is undoubtedly the largest media entertainment company in the world. In 2012 it did it again, breaking all box office record with Marvel's _Avengers Assemble_, which took $1.33bn (£855m) at box offices around the world, and became the third highest grossing film of all time behind _Avatar_ and _Titanic_.

It's safe to say that everyone in the world has seen a Disney movie, watched a Disney-owned TV channel, visited a Disney theme park, or bought a Disney toy or game. The company's hold over

▼ _Johnny Depp and Penelope Cruz, stars of_ Pirates of the Caribbean: On Stranger Tides.

the world of entertainment is impressively large, and still growing.

Despite its modern, forward-thinking outlook, the Walt Disney Company owes its success to the hard work and vision of two men, Roy Disney and particularly his younger brother Walt, who were born over 100 years ago into a very different world. Both men had a dream – to entertain children and their parents, and to capture and maintain the magic and wonder of childhood. And it all started with a mouse...

" *All our dreams can come true, if we have the courage to pursue them.* **"**
Walt Disney

▼ *Huge crowds walk down the main street of Eurodisney in Paris.*

▼ *This pie chart shows revenues for 2011 across the entire Walt Disney Company.*

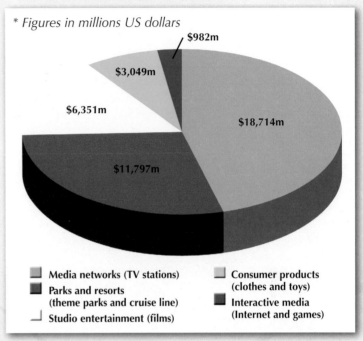

* Figures in millions US dollars

$982m
$3,049m
$6,351m
$18,714m
$11,797m

- ■ Media networks (TV stations)
- ■ Parks and resorts (theme parks and cruise line)
- ┘ Studio entertainment (films)
- ■ Consumer products (clothes and toys)
- ■ Interactive media (Internet and games)

The birth of Mickey Mouse

Today the Walt Disney Company spans the globe, but the origins of its founder and namesake are far more humble.

Walter Elias 'Walt' Disney was born on 5th December 1901, the youngest of five children. Young Walt spent his early years travelling the US, as his parents tried their luck at everything from gold prospecting to jam-making during the tough times of the American Depression. In his early teens, Walt became the cartoonist for his school newspaper in Chicago.

After leaving school he moved to Kansas City and found various jobs creating ads for newspapers and cinemas. At one of these, the Kansas City Film Ad Company, Walt produced early versions of TV commercials based on cut out animations. It sparked his own interest in animation and he started a company with colleague Fred Harman, producing cartoons called Laugh-O-Grams for a local cinema.

Unfortunately, Walt tried to grow his new company too quickly, hired too many animators, and went bust when new work failed to materialise. When the company closed, Walt and his older brother Roy put their savings together and moved to Hollywood – the film capital of the world! – to start a cartoon studio there.

⬆ *Brothers Walt (left) and Roy Disney (right) discuss a bank loan for their business with the Bank of America's Vice President Bernard Giannini (centre).*

The pair's first successful animated character was called Oswald the Lucky Rabbit, created in 1927. However they failed to trademark Oswald, and eventually lost the rights to produce Oswald cartoons to Universal Studios who had funded and produced the series.

Business Matters

Copyright law – 'Copyright' – basically the right to copy or reproduce something – gives the creators of certain types of media the right to control how their creations are used and distributed. Music, books, video and computer software all be covered by copyright law. However, when the creation of a new cartoon character or song, for example, is paid for by a corporation rather than by an individual, it is the corporation that holds the copyright, as happened with Disney and the Oswald character.

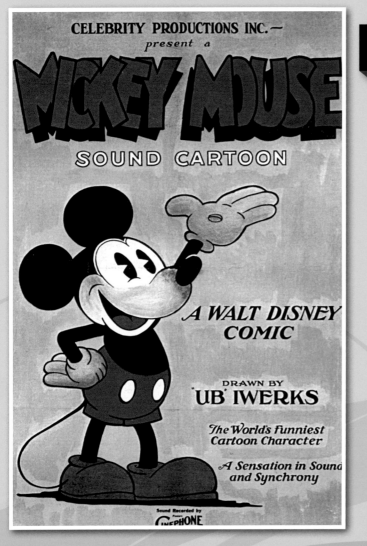

▲ *An early advert for a Mickey Mouse cartoon.*

Brains Behind The Brand

Walt Disney – co-founder, Walt Disney Productions
Walt was the dreamer, the risk taker, and the driving creative force behind Disney's animation studio, motion pictures, and the creation of the first Disneyland theme park in Anaheim, California (see page 12).

Like all the best company heads, Walt was extremely focussed on his audience, and the Disney brand. He knew that Disney should deliver wonder, excitement and family fun, and everything the company made or produced stuck to those principles. In fact Walt's vision was so strong, that the company still stays extremely close to his original ideals many years after his death.

Walt was determined to create a new character to replace Oswald, and came up with a mouse – based on one that lived in his Laugh-O-Gram studio in Kansas City that he had adopted as a pet! Walt called him Mickey Mouse.

After two silent animated films starring Mickey, Disney created a Mickey cartoon with sound called *Steamboat Willie*. Cartoonist Ubbe Iwerks, who Walt knew from his animation days in Kansas City, drew Mickey, and Walt himself provided Mickey's voice. The result was a huge success, and Mickey quickly became the world's most popular cartoon character. By 1932 The Mickey Mouse Club had one million members, and just two years later Mickey merchandise was making $600,000 (£386,000) per year.

Snow White and the seven Oscars

Like all great businessmen and innovators, Walt Disney wasn't content with just one success, he was always striving for bigger and better things.

Mickey Mouse was Disney's first major success, winning a special Academy Award in 1932 and launching a long list of new characters including Goofy, Pluto, and Donald Duck, who quickly rivalled Mickey for popularity and became successful in their own right.

However, when Walt announced his plan to produce a full-length animated version of the Snow White fairytale, the film industry thought he was mad, and even his brother Roy and Walt's wife Lillian tried to talk him out of it. Everyone thought the animation costs on a full-length film would be restrictively high, but Walt persevered with his plans. *Snow White and the*

Seven Dwarfs eventually went into production in 1934, and carried on until mid-1937 when Disney ran out of money. Undeterred by this setback, Walt took a rough cut of the film to the Bank of America to apply for a loan to finish the film!

The application was accepted, *Snow White* was finished and finally released in February 1938, becoming the most successful film of the year and earning over $8m (the equivalent of £122m today). The picture won an honorary Academy Award for screen innovation, and Walt was presented with an Oscar – and seven miniatures – to mark the achievement.

▼ *A scene from Disney's* Snow White and the Seven Dwarfs, *the world's first animated film.*

The profits from *Snow White* helped Disney build a huge new Walt Disney Studios complex in Burbank, California, which is still home to the company today. It also funded further full-length animations — *Pinocchio* and *Fantasia* were released in 1940, and *Dumbo* in 1941.

By December 1941, the United States had entered World War II. During the war production slowed dramatically as Disney and many of his animators were called up to help the war effort. By 1942, 90% of the company's 550 employees were working on war-related films. These films were great for morale, but didn't generate income for Disney, and by the end of the war, the studio's bank account was looking worryingly empty!

▼ *Walt's eight Oscars — one large and seven small — that he was awarded for* Snow White.

Brains Behind The Brand

Roy Disney – co-founder, Walt Disney Productions
If Walt was the creative force behind Disney, Roy was the businessman. Roy became Disney CEO in 1929, and shared the Chairman of the Board role with Walt until 1960.

Bringing Walt's visions to life cost a lot of money, and it was Roy's job to keep accurate accounts, make sure bills were paid, and ensure that the young company had enough money to pay its staff and invest in new projects. This role would probably have been given the title of Chief Financial Officer (CFO) in most companies.

When Walt died in 1966, Roy (who was 74 himself) came out of retirement to oversee completion of Walt Disney World, and ran the company until his own death in 1971.

> *All the adversity I've had in my life, all my troubles and obstacles, have strengthened me. You may not realise it when it happens, but a kick in the teeth may be the best thing in the world for you.*
> **Walt Disney**

Disney in your living room

Many companies occasionally suffer from cashflow problems. Often they have to change or adapt their plans to take these into account. In Disney's case, their problems led to further success.

After WWII, Disney and his animators returned to the studio full time. However, the war years had meant minimal film production, and therefore minimal income. It was clear that they didn't have the funds to start producing more full-length animated films straight away, so they concentrated on 'package films' (collections of already existing short films, edited together so that they could be sold into cinemas), as well as live-action films and documentaries, such as *Seal Island* (1948), which were cheaper to produce than animation.

By the end of the decade, Disney had recovered sufficiently to start work on several new animated films, *Alice In Wonderland* (1951), *Peter Pan* (1953), and *Cinderella* (1950), which became the company's most successful release since *Snow White*. Disney Studios also produced several successful live-action films throughout the 1950s, including *Treasure Island* (1950), *The Shaggy Dog* (1959) and *Swiss Family Robinson* (1960), and peaking with *Mary Poppins* in 1964, which won five Oscars, including Best Actress for Julie Andrews.

▼ *Walt Disney (left) discusses the soundtrack to* Fantasia *with the film's composer Deems Taylor (middle) and conductor Leopold Stokowski (right).*

▲ *A still from Disney's* Song of the South, *which mixed live action with animation.*

However, it was the rise of television that really provided Disney's biggest new opportunities for growth. In 1950, Walt Disney Productions and the Coca-Cola Company teamed up to produce a one-hour special for NBC television, called *An Hour In Wonderland*. New opportunities to find Disney fans in every living room in the US opened up to Walt, and by 1954 Disney launched its *Disneyland* series on ABC, a mixture of live action and animation that gave Disney the chance to raid its archive as well as introduce new characters and ideas.

By 1955, the studio's first daily show, *Mickey Mouse Club*, launched on ABC. Produced under Walt's direct supervision, it was a groundbreaking mix of comedy, music and drama aimed completely at children. Walt even went back into the studio himself to record Mickey Mouse's voice. The show was a huge success, running around the world for many years, and even appearing on the Disney Channel into the 1990s, where it launched the careers of the singers Britney Spears, Christina Aguilera and Justin Timberlake and the actor Ryan Gosling.

Business Matters

Diversification — companies often decide to offer new products or services — as when Disney moved into television production — because it reduces the risk of its other business interests becoming too limited or uninteresting. By adding television production to its animation studio, Disney gave consumers more reasons to engage with the Disney brand. When companies offer a completely different product or service, like supermarkets offering car or house insurance, this is called 'brandstretching'.

▼ *This pie chart shows income from subscription channels by value in US dollars.*

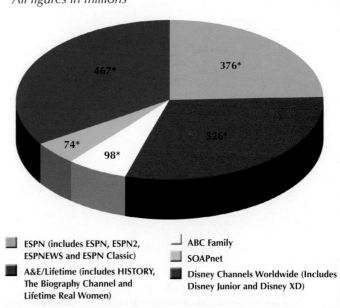

* All figures in millions

467* 376* 526* 74* 98*

■ ESPN (includes ESPN, ESPN2, ESPNEWS and ESPN Classic)

■ A&E/Lifetime (includes HISTORY, The Biography Channel and Lifetime Real Women)

─ ABC Family

■ SOAPnet

■ Disney Channels Worldwide (Includes Disney Junior and Disney XD)

The birth of the theme parks

Since the late 1940s, Walt had been dreaming up ideas for an amusement park that adults could enjoy as much as their children. The project became known as Disneyland.

A great believer in family entertainment, Walt became fascinated with the idea of a theme park where his employees could take their children and enjoy time together. He was inspired by the opening of the Children's Fairyland in Oakland, California and initially planned to build his own park on vacant land across the road from the Disney offices in Burbank.

As usual, Walt's plans grew more and more ambitious and cost estimates started to rise. To safeguard the finances of Walt Disney Productions, Walt and Roy created a new company, WED Enterprises, that would carry out planning and production for the park. A carefully selected group of Disney studio employees also joined the project as engineers and planners, and were nicknamed 'the Imagineers'.

Walt and Roy succeeded in winning television network ABC's financial backing for the project and in 1955 – after five years of building – the Disneyland Park in Anaheim, California opened to the public. On the opening day, 18 July 1955, Walt gave a speech:

'Disneyland is dedicated to the ideals, the dreams and the hard facts that have created America... with the hope that it will be a source of joy and inspiration to all the world.'

▼ *Sleeping Beauty's Castle under construction at Disneyland in 1955.*

Brains Behind The Brand

Thomas Staggs – Chairman, Walt Disney Parks and Resorts

Staggs oversees Disney's worldwide holiday and travel business, which includes a cruise line, holiday resorts, and 11 theme parks in five locations across the US, Europe and Asia. He took over the role in January 2010, and was previously Disney's Chief Financial Officer (CFO), in charge of areas including worldwide finances and company acquisitions (see page 25).

Staggs joined Disney in 1990 as Manager of Strategic Planning, becoming CFO in 1998. He played a major part in Disney's acquisitions of TV network Capital Cities/ABC, and film studios Pixar and Marvel.

Demand grew for Disney theme parks around the world, and in April 1992 Disneyland Paris opened to the public. The cost of building parks is extremely high, and Disney usually shares the costs – and therefore the ownership – with a local partner. Disney owns 39.78% of Disneyland Paris shares, and 43% of the shares in Shanghai Disney Resort, a $4.4bn development in China that is due to launch in December 2015.

The opportunity for Disney fans around the world to experience Walt's dream firsthand is a huge part of what makes the brand so successful and loved.

> " Disneyland is a work of love. We didn't go into Disneyland just with the idea of making money. "
>
> **Walt Disney**

Disneyland is divided into several different worlds, with a stylised and nostalgic vision of America that adults love, and funfair rides that are exciting enough to challenge everyone's courage. Add to that the appearance, several times a day, of life-size Disney characters, from Mickey Mouse to Tigger, and it's not surprising that Disneyland now attracts around 16m visitors per year.

By 1965 Disney was ready to expand, and plans to launch 'Disney World' in Orlando, Florida, were announced. Walt Disney World today contains four theme parks, two water parks, 23 on-site hotels and five golf courses, and is the world's most visited entertainment resort with close to 17m visitors per year to its Magic Kingdom.

Mickey and Minnie Mouse in traditional dress at Tokyo's Disneyland.

Life and death at Disney

Some companies are built around the vision and personality of one man – like Steve Jobs at Apple, or Walt at Disney. Yet they also need to survive after the death of their founder and figurehead.

On 2 November 1966, Walt underwent X-rays before routine surgery on an old neck injury. Doctors discovered a tumour on his left lung, and further tests showed it to be malignant. Walt underwent emergency surgery and chemotherapy, and returned home to recuperate. Unfortunately, on 30 November he collapsed at his home and on 15 December, just ten days after his 65th birthday, he died.

Before his illness, Walt had been as busy as ever. He was supervising construction of Disney World Resort in Florida, plans for a new ski resort in Sequoia National Forest, and renovations of Disneyland in Anaheim, as well as six motion pictures, and countless television productions.

Throughout his life, Walt held no formal title at Disney, but he was unquestionably the boss. Under his leadership, Disney had won 29 Oscars and four Emmys, and Walt himself had been awarded the Presidential Freedom Medal. Nevertheless, brother Roy was determined to carry on the Disney legacy as smoothly as possible. In 1967 he released the final two films with which Walt had been actively involved, the musical *The Happiest Millionaire* and *The Jungle Book*.

Mowgli with friends Baloo the bear and Bagheera the panther in a scene from The Jungle Book.

> **" "** We will continue to operate Walt's company in the way that he had established and guided it. All of the plans for the future that Walt had begun will continue to move ahead. **" "**
>
> *Roy Disney*

▲ *The entire staff of Walt Disney World pose for a photograph before the grand opening of the theme park in 1971.*

Roy also kept Walt's amusement park dream alive and saw through plans to finish the Florida theme park. Walt Disney World, named in Walt's honour, was opened in October 1971. Two months later Roy died from a stroke and the running of the company passed to long-time Disney executives Donn Tatum and Card Walker, both trained by Roy and Walt.

Management continuity is often important for large businesses, and when Donn Tatum became Disney CEO after Roy's death, he had already worked at Disney for 15 years. So despite being the first non-Disney family member to be company president, he was well trained in the core values of Disney. Tatum played an important role in the development of the Walt Disney World Resort and EPCOT Center in Florida, as well as Tokyo Disneyland. Card Walker had been with Disney even longer, joining the company's post room in 1938! Between Tatum and Walker, they were at the head of Disney until 1983.

▼ *For a company as well-established as Disney, it has had very few Presidents since its launch in 1923.*

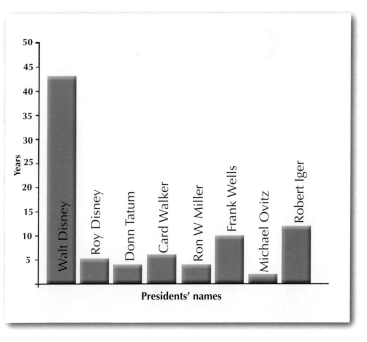

The wonderful world of Disney

The theme parks are the public face of Disney. But it's the Walt Disney Studios in Burbank that are the real heart of the Disney empire, housing management offices, film stages and animation studios.

When Walt and Roy Disney moved to Los Angeles in the summer of 1923, they set up their first office in the garage of their Uncle Robert in an area called Los Feliz. By 1925, with distribution secured on a new animated series called *Alice Comedies*, Walt invested in larger office space at 2719 Hyperion Avenue. By 1940, they were ready to move again, and Walt reinvested the profits from *Snow White* to build the Walt Disney Studios in Burbank.

There are around 15,000 employees (Disney prefers to call them 'cast members') working at the Walt Disney Studios. This includes animators, set builders, office staff, film producers, TV executives and many more. The site contains many of the original animation buildings from the 1940s, as well as sound stages (warehouse-sized, soundproof buildings where films are made), staff offices and restaurants.

Current president and CEO of Disney, Robert Iger, has an office in the Michael D Eisner Building, which is named after the former head of Disney who ran the company for 21 years. Alongside Iger, there are offices for Rich Ross, Chairman of the Walt Disney Studios, Thomas Staggs, Chairman of Walt Disney Parks, and Andy Bird, Chairman of Walt Disney International.

Outside the Eisner Building is the Disney Legends Plaza, containing statues of Walt with Mickey Mouse, and Roy with Minnie. Bronze plaques commemorate valued Disney animators and 'Imagineers', with their hand prints and signatures set into the bronze.

Across from the Plaza is the Frank G Wells Building, named after the former Disney President. The Wells Building houses Disney's TV animation department, the company archives (a museum of Disney memorabilia) and the Human Resources (HR) department.

▼ *An aerial view of the Walt Disney Studios in Burbank, California.*

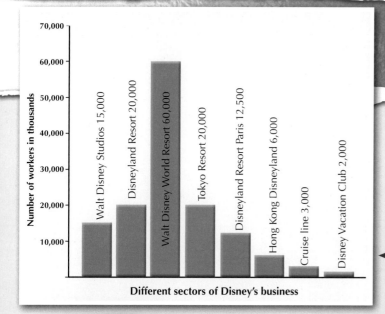

This graph shows the number of workers or 'cast members' who were employed in the various sectors of Disney's business in 2011.

Cast members usually eat lunch in one of the two restaurants on site. The Studio Commissary serves chilli every day in memory of Walt, who often came in for a bowl, even of the hottest of California days. There is also a Starbucks coffee shop and a Disney Store for cast members only!

Business Matters

Human Resources — The Human Resources (HR) department of a company is responsible for putting in place and maintaining the business practices that allow effective people management. Some key responsibilities of an HR department are: 1) training; 2) staff appraisal: a formal process, performed by managers on their staff, which aims to communicate how they are performing and to discuss what they need in order to improve and develop; 3) staff development: the processes in the company designed to identify the people with potential, keep them in the organization, and move them into the right positions.

Animator Marc Segan, with early Disney artwork from 'Steamboat Willie'.

Disney grows up

By the 1980s it was clear that Disney needed to modernise and bring in new blood to face the business challenges ahead. A failed takeover attempt was just the motivation they needed to make changes fast!

Throughout the 1970s and early 1980s, Disney carried on producing a mix of animated and live action films, including the futuristic *Tron* in 1982. Its success led to then Disney CEO Ron Miller, Walt's son-in-law, creating a new brand, Touchstone Pictures, which could release more adult-oriented films, like *Splash* (1984) with Tom Hanks.

In 1983, Disney launched the subscription-only Disney Channel, featuring its archive of classic films and TV shows. Works also continued with Walt's dream for a space-age city, which became the EPCOT Center in Florida.

Despite the success of the Disney Channel and its theme parks, Disney was falling behind its Hollywood competitors, and the management team, led by 50-year old Miller, was often criticised for lacking vision and ambition. In 1984, a US

⬆ *Jeffrey Katzenberg (left) and Michael Eisner at the opening of Disney's Beauty and the Beast.*

businessman called Saul Steinberg launched a 'hostile takeover' bid with the aim of buying Disney and selling off its various parts – theme parks, movie archive and so on– to the highest bidders.

Disney managed to fight off the bid thanks to friendly investors, but the management, including Roy's son, Roy E Disney, realised that they needed to strengthen the management team and plan for the future, and so hired Michael Eisner and Jeffrey Katzenberg from Paramount Pictures, and Frank Wells from Warner Brothers.

Business Matters

Company directors – Company directors, often called a board of directors, oversee the activities of a company. A board's role is determined by the powers and responsibilities given to it by a company's own rules and regulations. These rules usually cover the number of members of the board, how they are chosen, and how often they meet. The board usually chooses one of its members to be the Chairman (or 'President' in the US). Typical duties of a board include: setting the rules that run the organization; selecting, appointing, supporting and reviewing the performance of the chief executive; approving annual budgets; reporting to shareholders on the company's performance.

Brains Behind The Brand

Rich Ross – Chairman, the Walt Disney Studios

Ross oversees all new production from the Pixar, Marvel and Disney film studios, as well as marketing and distribution for the independent DreamWorks Studios. In recent years, this has included massive global hits from Disney's *Alice in Wonderland and Pirates of the Caribbean: On Stranger Tides* to Marvel's *Avengers Assemble*.

Before joining Disney Studios in 2009, Ross was President of Disney Channels Worldwide, and was responsible for original programmes such as *Hannah Montana, High School Musical, Phineas and Ferb* and *Wizards of Waverley Place*, which contributed to a massive growth in Disney's TV business.

The new management team brought the dynamism and energy to Disney that had been lacking for a few years. Under Michael Eisner's management from 1984-2005, Disney experienced strong growth and consolidation, starting with the successes of films *Who Framed Roger Rabbit* (1988), which won three Oscars, including for best visual effects and sound effects editing, and *The Little Mermaid* (1989).

At the start of the 1990s, Eisner announced plans for 'The Disney Decade', which included existing park expansions, new parks being built, new film franchises and new media investments.

Over the next few years, Disney bought Miramax Pictures in 1993, released the Oscar-winning *The Lion King* (1994), merged with Capital Cities/ABC on the TV side in 1996 (which brought in ABC and ESPN sports network), and launched new theme parks in Hong Kong and Paris. When Eisner finally stepped down in 2005, his role was taken by his long-time assistant, Robert Iger – once again ensuring continuity within the company.

◄ In 1994, 'Can you feel the love tonight' from The Lion King won the Oscar for best song for Elton John (left) and Tim Rice (right).

'The best 30 minutes of a child's day'

When the first Disney Store opened in 1987, Disney finally entered the world of retail. Fortunes have risen and fallen over the years, but now appear to be back on top.

The first Disney Store opened in Glendale, California in March 1987. The idea was so successful that the company quickly expanded to over 600 stores around the world. However, in some cases, Disney opened as many as five stores in the same town, and sales just couldn't keep up with store running costs. By 2002, Disney stores were losing around $100m (£64m) per year.

Large and successful companies will often support a division that is losing money, but Disney management decided instead to license the business, which means they sold the rights to use the Disney name to another company. The Children's Place, who bought the licence, had to operate under strict rules laid down by Disney regarding the merchandise they sold in Disney Stores, and the prices they charged.

Unfortunately, the partnership was not a success. The Children's Place believed it could not run the business in the way it wanted to and Disney did not feel that the stores accurately reflected the Disney brand. So in 2008, Disney 'bought back' its own stores, closing some of the less successful ones in the chain.

When Disney bought Pixar Studios in 2006, they granted a place on their board of directors to

▼ *A trademark Disney Store, decorated for Christmas.*

▲ *Bob Chapek (fourth on the right) with cast members at a party to celebrate a Hollywood screening of* High School Musical.

Steve Jobs, Pixar's owner and the man who had revitalised the fortunes of computer company Apple and launched the extremely successful Apple stores.

With Jobs' help, the President of Disney Stores, Jim Fielding, announced a five-year plan to turn the Disney shopping experience into 'the best 30 minutes of a child's day'. It's estimated that Disney will spend $1m (£640,000) per store to modernise its whole chain. Stores will include 'Magic Mirrors' that speak to children holding princesses' tiaras, and interactive displays will show Disney films and TV shows on touch-screens.

Brains Behind The Brand

Bob Chapek – President, Disney Consumer Products (DCP)

Disney has its name and images on more products than any other company in the world – from clothes, toys and stationery to food, drink and home furnishings. Chapek oversees this large and complicated business, which includes Walt Disney Studios, Pixar and now Marvel Comics. His job is to maximise revenues while ensuring that products are good quality and meet customers' needs.

Chapek became President of Consumer Products in 2011 after two years as President of Distribution for Walt Disney Studios, where he was involved in overseeing new movies through cinema releases, onto DVD, then subscription channels and new media. In this role he set several sales records in the straight-to-video business that included *High School Musical* and its sequels.

Business Matters

Long-term success — successful companies are 'market-driven', in other words they focus on satisfying the exact section of the market in which they are operating. All of Disney's different companies — from television to theme parks — have to make sure that they provide something that visitors or viewers ('the market') want. Successful companies also need to be 'sustainable', meaning that people not only want to buy or use their products now, but that they will continue to want to use them in the future.

Disney gets interactive

Interactive entertainment – another name for computer and social media games – is an important part of Disney's business strategy, helping the company connect with fans through their game consoles and now mobile phones.

Disney followed the explosion in the video games industry in the 1980s by launching its own division to focus on the development of computer and video games, Walt Disney Computer Software, in 1988.

At first, Disney worked mainly as a games developer, coding and designing new games featuring Disney cartoon and film characters, and relying on business agreements with games publishers such as Sony, Nintendo and others to manufacture and distribute the games.

In 2003, Disney's games division brought production and distribution in-house, and rebranded as Buena Vista Games. One part of the company, Buena Vista Interactive, focussed on multi-platform games for teens and adults, while Disney Interactive specialised in children's entertainment and learning software. Buena Vista Games' biggest success was a series of action role-playing games called *Kingdom Hearts*, which has sold 17 million copies worldwide and launched spin-off magazines, figurines and even a music soundtrack.

◄ *The Disney Dreamsketcher, just one of many Disney interactive toys and games.*

As cinema audiences began to reduce and CD sales kept falling, interactive games companies have become more profitable than the traditional entertainment areas of film and music. Games developers such as Take-Two Interactive (who produce the *Bioshock* and *Grand Theft Auto* series) are generating revenues of over $1bn (£640m) per year, and social games developer Zynga, which makes games like *FarmVille* and *CityVille*, which can be played on mobile phones or through users' Facebook pages, makes over $600m (£383m) per year.

Disney's games division was keen to take a slice of this growing market, and rebranded again in 2007, becoming Disney Interactive Media Group (DIMG - pronounced 'dim-gee'). In 2010, it purchased Playdom, a successful social game developer with 47 million monthly users, for over $500m (£320m).

▼ Despite growing revenues, DIMG has made a loss every year since its launch.

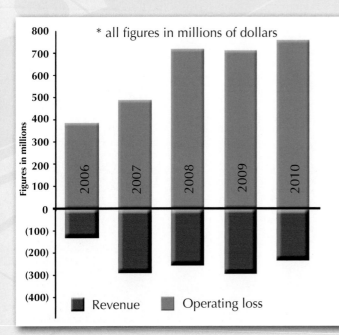

Despite the investment in Playdom, DIMG is currently one of Disney's few non-profitable divisions. Since January 2011 it has made over 200 employees redundant, and in the first three months of 2012, announced a $28m (£17.8m) loss. DIMG is now shifting production away from expensive console games towards online and mobile gaming, but only time will tell if it will bring success to what is still a troubled Disney division.

Brains Behind The Brand

John Pleasants – Co-President, Disney Interactive Media Group

Pleasants runs two Disney divisions – DIMG, the interactive entertainment section that focuses on console and mobile games, and Playdom, which produced Disney's social media games. He oversees the creation and development of all new games, and is in regular contact with Disney's global network of game developers to make sure that he gets the best, must-buy products first.

Pleasants was previously the CEO of Playdom, which was bought by Disney in 2010. Before joining Playdom, he was President of Publishing and Chief Operating Officer (COO) of games company Electronic Arts, where he was in charge of global sales. Pleasants has also worked at major websites Ticketmaster and Match.com.

Steadying the ship

Under current CEO and Chairman Bob Iger, Disney has continued to grow and prosper, keeping its connections with the company's rich traditions, but always looking to the future.

Since Iger took over from Michael Eisner, Disney has gone through a period of modernising and adapting to the changes in consumer tastes. This has meant embracing the possibilities of computer animation and 3D film-making, and moving away from Disney's hand-drawn animation. 'I really believe the company should look at technology as a friend,' explains Iger. 'It had been part of the company originally. Walt Disney was a big believer in technology.'

Iger's first step was to invest in the company's long-term film-making success, buying Pixar for $7.4bn (£4.7bn) in 2006, and Marvel Entertainment for $4.2bn (£2.7bn) in 2009. Both studios focussed on the strong storytelling and family-friendly releases that have always been Disney's trademark. At the same time, the Miramax and Touchstone brands were sold or downsized, and the company's loss-making divisions (like DIMG) were also cut back.

More recently, Iger has made positive steps to tap into the fast-growing Far East market, working hard to secure the support of the Chinese government to start work on the Shanghai Disney Resort, which is scheduled to open in 2015. In 2012, Disney bought UTV Software

◄ *An artist's impression of a completed Shanghai Disney Resort, scheduled to open in 2015.*

▲ Iron Man *was a big cinema hit for Disney in 2008.*

Communications, an Indian multimedia company, producing films, TV, website, games and animation, in order to keep expanding Disney's business into Asia.

With over 160 million members of Disney Facebook groups, Iger has taken the opportunity to engage with these fans, find out what they are thinking, and use their feedback for valuable market research. Iger is as big a Disney fan as any of them, but he realises that the company is competing in the 21st century, and that simply 'doing what Walt did' is not going to take the company to further success.

Disney today is at the height of its powers. The challenge now for Iger, and the whole company, is to keep growing and keep innovating, while staying faithful to the ideals that makes Disney such a magical, well-loved brand.

Brains Behind The Brand

Robert Iger – Chairman and CEO, the Walt Disney Company
As Chairman of Disney, Iger is responsible for one of the world's best-loved brands. His job is to keep the company growing and thriving, but every decision he makes is based on three important principles: generating the best content possible; innovating and using the latest technology available; expanding into new markets around the world.

With the purchase of Pixar in 2006 and Marvel Comics in 2009, Iger has remained loyal to Walt Disney's goal of focussing on great storytelling. He has also helped make the company an industry leader in creating content across multiple platforms – from cinema and DVD to mobile phones and tablets.

Iger began his career in 1974 with US television channel ABC, and worked his way to the top, becoming chairman of ABC in 1996. In 1999 he was promoted to President, Walt Disney International, then Chairman and CEO in 2005.

Business Matters

Mergers and acquisitions — This phrase refers to the aspect of company strategy and finance that deals with the buying, selling and combining of different companies. This strategy can help a company grow rapidly within its market without having to create another separate company. An acquisition is the purchase of one company by another company, as when Disney bought Pixar in 2006 and Playdom in 2010. A merger is when two companies combine to form a third, new company.

Business success is based on constantly moving forward – assessing what works and doesn't work, and acting accordingly. Here's how we predict Disney will change in the next few years.

It's safe to assume that Disney will focus its efforts on several key areas, as follows:

Film franchises
Disney's huge success with the first *Avengers* movie is sure to lead to further Marvel films. The Marvel Studios President, Kevin Feige, has announced that two new films will go into production, *Iron Man 3* and *Thor 2*. They will be followed by the second *Captain America* film, and an inevitable *Avengers* sequel. There are also new Marvel adaptations promised, including *Guardians of the Galaxy* and *Ant-Man*.

International expansion
Disney has already taken the significant step of starting work on a new theme park in Shanghai, which it plans to open by 2015. There are also plans to open a smaller park in Haifa, Israel. Hong Kong Disneyland has announced that three new 'lands' will be added to the park – Grizzly Gulch, Mystic Point and Toy Story Land.

◄ *In 2011 Disney released The Muppets, starring Jason Segel and Amy Adams. The film made over $100 million worldwide.*

❝ *'If you can dream it, you can do it.'* **Walt Disney** ❞

Brains Behind The Brand

Andy Bird - Chairman, Walt Disney International

Bird has three main areas of responsibility: targeting existing businesses for Disney to buy; increasing Disney's market share and profitability in the main markets of Western Europe and Japan; and leading Disney's development into new, 'emerging' markets like India, China and Russia.

Bird joined Disney in 2004, and one of his first deals was the purchase of Indian TV station Hungama TV in order to grow Disney's visibility in the region. He has also worked for global TV and entertainment company Time Warner, where he was in charge of their TV channels.

Updating US parks

In September 2011, Disney secured exclusive global theme parks rights to director James Cameron's *Avatar*. Plans were immediately announced to partner with 20th Century Fox, and Cameron's production company, Lightstorm Entertainment, to build theme park attractions based on the blockbusting film. The first ride is planned for Disney's Animal Kingdom at Walt Disney World, Florida. The park is also due for further new rides, including a *Little Mermaid* ride, and a *Seven Dwarfs' Mine Train* ride.

More cruise line destinations

Disney will also focus on its holiday and resort business, and are planning to add a new cruise – from Los Angeles to Hawaii – to their itinerary. They are also adding new home ports in New York City and Galveston, making it easier for passengers to join Atlantic and Caribbean cruises.

Advances in technology

Disney will undoubtedly use advances in technology to attract and engage new fans. New apps will allow Disney Channel subscribers to watch the Disney Channel, Disney XD and Disney Junior on their handheld devices. DIMG's focus will also be on building an online community of loyal Disney fans that will grow up with the brand, just as children have been doing since the 1930s.

Although no company's continued success is ever guaranteed, Disney's future looks to be in safe hands. Here's to the next 100 years!

◀ *Disney Stores worldwide are being modernised and made more interactive.*

To create a new product, it is helpful to produce a product development brief like the one below. This is a sample brief for a new theme park ride called Iron Man. The SWOT analysis on the page opposite will help you to think about the strengths, weaknesses, opportunities and threats for your product. This can help you to see how feasible and practical your idea is before you think of investing time and money in it.

Product Development Brief

Name of product: Iron Man 'Total Experience' Ride

Type of product: Theme park ride for Disney resorts worldwide

The product explained (use 25 words or less): This new ride brings the Iron Man movies to life – experience flying and super strength in your own Iron Man bodysuit.

Target age of users: 15-45

What does the product do? This ride is actually a simulator, but instead of placing all participants into a rollercoaster carriage in front of a video screen, each person using Iron Man puts on their own suit, and has the video screen projected onto the inside of the goggles they are wearing. Additional movements are made by standing on a motion simulator and operating pressure points from inside the suit.

Are there any similar products already available? None

What makes your product different? It's the first motion simulator 'ride' that gives the passenger the experience of being fully immersed in a game.

Name of product you are assessing . . . Iron Man 'Total Experience' Ride

The table below will help you assess your Disney theme park ride. By addressing all four areas, you can make your product stronger and more likely to be a success.

Questions to consider

Does your ride do something unique?

Is there anything innovative about it?

What are its USPs (unique selling points)?

Strengths

It's the only ride of its kind in the world.

Simulator rides and using goggles are not new, but no one has provided a full immersion simulation for the price of a theme park ride.

Why wouldn't people use this ride?

Can everyone use it?

Are there any dangers associated with the ride?

Do you need additional trained members of staff to monitor customers when they use the ride in case they have problems with it?

Weaknesses

The Iron Man 'Total Experience' will have age limits and height restrictions. It may also require a basic health check, and perhaps blood pressure to be taken, before park visitors can use it.

Some users may experience motion sickness.

Iron Man suits are expensive to make, and so only limited numbers will be available at each park. Therefore queues could be very long to be able to use one.

Can the ride be improved in the future, eg better graphics, or motion simulation?

Can the ride be used at Disney parks worldwide?

Can it develop new USPs?

Opportunities

As technology gets even more realistic, and cheaper to produce, the ride can become better, and cheaper over time.

Theme parks worldwide can use the suit, as there are no language barriers.

New technology advances could introduce new experiences to the suit, eg feeling hot, cold, wind on the skin, that would improve the experience.

Is the market that you are selling in to shrinking?

Will the ride face competition from other theme parks?

Are any of your weaknesses so bad they might affect the ride in the long run?

Threats

No, the market will keep growing.

Other parks will develop rides based on other blockbuster films.

The technology will be untried at first, and may well experience breakdowns and leave suits out of action. Hopefully they can be fixed quickly, or customers will lose confidence in the ride.

Do you have what it takes to work at Disney?
Try this!

1. Are you a fan of cartoons and animation?

a) No, cartoons are for little kids! I left that behind at pre-school.

b) I like *Spongebob Square Pants*. Does that count?

c) Yes, love it! I think animation can be a fun and immediate way of telling a story to all generations.

2. Do you like theme parks and theme park rides?

a) Ooh, they're too scary for me! I like to keep my feet on the ground.

b) I've been to the odd one on school trips, and I try to visit new rides when they open.

c) Yes, I've even been to Walt Disney World in Florida. It's magical. I can't wait to go back!

3. When was the last time you went to the cinema?

a) I'm not a big cinemagoer. I prefer watching football, or playing video games at home.

b) I go 5-6 times a year – usually with a big group of friends. We enjoy the experience of being together as much as the films we watch.

c) I go all the time! I keep up with all the latest releases – especially action and fantasy films.

4) Have you ever come up with an idea that you thought would make a great film?

a) Mmm, I prefer hearing other people's ideas rather than coming up with my own.

b) I sometimes read books and think they would make great films. *Hunger Games*, for example!

c) I did actually have a great idea for a story with loads of new characters that I think people would love. Help me get it made into a film!

5. What's your favourite subject at school?

a) Food technology. Oh, and I like Games.

b) Probably history. I enjoy learning about old civilisations and how people lived in ancient times.

c) I enjoy English. Creative writing is a big favourite of mine. I love coming up with fantastic ideas about interesting people.

6. What do you want to do when you leave school?

a) I'm planning to work for the family business. That way I can take days off whenever I want and not get sacked.

b) I want to go to university, and then hopefully become a teacher.

c) I'd love to work for a big global corporation that affects millions of people's lives. I'm prepared to work very hard to get to the top!

Results

Mostly As: Sorry, but your chances of working at Disney are looking shaky! It doesn't sound like you have the interest in Disney's main business areas to succeed at this world-famous company.

Mostly Bs: You are thoughtful and hard-working, but you need to work on your motivation and individuality if you want to succeed in a very competitive business.

Mostly Cs: It sounds like you have what it takes to get a job at Disney. Keep working hard at school, and pushing to be the best, and who knows?

adaptation film versions of a book, or comic book.

archive a collection of older programmes that can be reused or re-edited.

bumper exceptionally large or successful.

cashflow the amount of money a company has in the bank at a given time.

coffers the funds or financial reserves of a company.

commemorating recalling or showing respect to something or someone.

computer chip an electronic circuit that forms the basis of many electronic devices.

core values most deeply or passionately held beliefs.

downsized made a company smaller by reducing staff numbers.

dynamism positivity, hard-working attitude.

embracing willingly or enthusiastically accepting something.

franchise a well-known or important brand name, for example *The Avengers*, which can make money in different media, from films, games, merchandise and so on.

futuristic involving modern or advanced technology.

grossing a figure without costs (for example production costs) taken off. Film can gross £100m, but if they cost £120m to make, then they lose money!

honorary a special award to recognise achievement.

humble modest, unimportant, unimpressive.

inevitable certain to happen, unavoidable.

initially at first.

innovator someone who introduces new methods, ideas or products into an existing business.

instalment a part of something, for example one film in a series about the same character or characters.

itinerary a planned route or journey.

malignant describes a tumour that is spreading.

materialise to happen, become real

merchandise products used to promote a film, cartoon character, etc. Can include posters, action figures and so on.

minimal a small or insignificant amount.

modernise to adapt or change something for modern tastes or interests.

net profits profits after all costs have been taken into account.

nostalgic feeling happy memories about the past, or one's childhood

persevere to keep trying with little or no chance of success.

revenue income, money coming in to a company.

strive to make great efforts to achieve something.

subscription a membership or monthly payment.

trademark to legally register the ownership of something.

undeterred persevering with something despite setbacks.

went bust went bankrupt, lost all one's money.

Academy Awards 8, 9, 10, 14

acquisitions 13, 25

Andrews, Julie 10

animation 6, 7, 8, 9, 10, 11, 14, 16, 18, 24

characters 8, 9, 11, 13, 22

copyright law 6

Depp, Johnny 4

Disney brand 7, 11, 13, 25, 27

Disney, Roy 5, 6, 8, 9, 12, 14, 15, 16, 18

Disney Stores 17, 18, 19

Disney, Walt 4, 5, 6, 7, 8, 9, 10, 11, 12, 14, 15, 16, 17, 18, 24, 25

diversification 11

Eisner, Michael 18, 19

films 4, 6, 7, 8, 9, 10, 14, 16, 18, 19, 21, 24, 26

human resources (HR) 17

Iger, Robert 15, 16, 19, 24, 25

interactive entertainment 22, 23, 27

Jobs, Steve 14, 20

Katzenberg, Jeffrey 18

merchandise 5, 7

mergers 25

Mickey Mouse 5, 6, 7, 8, 11

revenues 4, 5, 7, 21, 22, 23

social media games 22, 23

Tatum, Donn 15

television 4, 5, 11, 12, 13, 18, 19, 21, 27

theme parks 4, 5, 7, 12, 13, 14, 15, 16, 18, 19, 21, 26, 27

Walker, Card 15

Walt Disney Studios 9, 10, 16, 17, 21

Wells, Frank 15, 18

World War II 9, 10

BIG BU$INE$$

Contents of all the titles in the series:

Apple
978 0 7502 7090 8

An Apple in every home
The origins of Apple
Building the Apple brand
Fallout at the top
Steve returns to Apple
Riding the Internet wave
Apple explores music
The invention of the iPhone
There's an app for that!
Apple takes on publishing
What makes Apple so 'must-have'?
What does the future hold for Apple?
Design your own App for the App Store!
Do you have what it takes to work at Apple?

Disney
978 0 7502 6922 3

Disney on top
The birth of Mickey Mouse
Snow White and the Seven Oscars
Disney in your living room
The birth of the theme park
Life and death at Disney
The wonderful world of Disney
Disney grows up
A store in every town
Disney Interactive
Steadying the ship
What does the future hold for Disney?
Design your own Disney venture
Do you have what it takes to work at Disney?

Microsoft
978 0 7502 6924 7

Riding high
From small beginnings
The launch of MS-DOS
Opening Windows, 1983
'A computer on every desk'
Bill Gates: the man behind Microsoft
The Internet takes off
New Windows to the world
Entering the games world: Xbox
Into the clouds
Microsoft in the community
Microsoft's vision
Develop your own Microsoft product
Do you have what it takes to work at Microsoft?

Cadbury
978 0 7502 6923 0

Sweet success
The founder: John Cadbury
Building the business 1861-1900
Philanthropy: a helping hand
Enter Dairy Milk 1900-20
Facing the competition 1920-45
Business booms 1945-69
A Cadbury world
Cadbury Schweppes 1969-89
New markets, new products 1990-2010
Purple goes green
The end of an era
Design your own Cadbury venture
Do you have what it takes to work at Cadbury?

Facebook
978 0 7502 7088 5

Birth of a new brand
Facebook Inc
The site at a glance
The idea keeps on growing
An expert on board
Making popularity pay
To high school and beyond
Going global
The secret to making money
There's more to Facebook than friends
To share or not to share?
What's next for Facebook?
Invent your own Facebook app
Do you have what it takes to work at Facebook?

Nike
978 0 7502 6925 4

Nike rules the world
The birth of the business
Growing the company
Better by design
The Nike brand is born
First hiccups
Built on innovation
Star power
Life at Nike HQ
Coming through adversity
Going global
What does the future hold for Nike?
Do you have what it takes to work at Nike?

Coca-Cola
978 0 7502 6921 6

Coca-Cola at the top
'A delicious and refreshing beverage'
Coke and the American way of life
New-look Coke - the 'real thing'
Coke and sports
New markets, new drinks
Coca-Cola controversies
Coca-Cola: a marketing miracle
The challenge of sustainability
Corporate social responsibility (CSR)
Muhtar Kent, head of Coca-Cola
'2020 Vision': Coca-Cola's future
Design your own Coca-Cola venture
Do you have what it takes to work at Coca Cola?

Google
978 0 7502 7089 2

The world gets Googled!
What makes Google so good?
Google is born
Setting up the company
Standing out from the competition
Making a profit
Keeping the staff happy
Google goes public
Expanding the business
Diversifying the business
Google changes the world
Making Google future-proof
Invent the next Google product!
Do you have what it takes to work at Google?

Nintendo
978 0 7502 7091 5

Nintendo rules the world!
Seizing the opportunity
From playing cards to electronics
Building a reputation for fun
The Game Boy arrives!
The battle for your living room
The business of games creation
Expanding the games market
Mario – the superstar 30 years!
Games the whole family can play
Games for everyday life
Making plans for the future
Invent a new Nintendo game!
Do you have what it takes to work at Nintendo?